...es of America

AMERICAN
BIRDING SKETCHBOOK

LANGFORD PRESS 2012

Colorado - April
The drama of a Sage Grouse lek — the display of these
superb creatures in the mountain flanked sage-brush, was
a brilliant and memorable experience.

AMERICAN
BIRDING SKETCHBOOK
MICHAEL WARREN

American Woodcock -
Virginia - May

Text © Michael Warren
Foreword © Robert Bateman
Illustrations © Michael Warren

Langford Press, 10 New Road,
Langtoft, Peterborough, PE6 9LE
www.langford-press.co.uk

Designed by Simon Warren
Printed in Spain under the supervision
of MRM Graphics Ltd, Winslow.

A CIP Record for this book is
available from the British Library
ISBN 978-1-904078-47-0

For the late Jim Helzer

Acknowledgements

This book is dedicated to the late Jim Helzer of Unicover Corporation, Cheyenne, Wyoming. Without Jim's interest in my work and the subsequent projects we developed. this book would not have been possible.

Thanks go to my wife Kate, son Simon and daughter Clara. They visited swamps; mosquito infested mud flats, tick ridden grasslands. They were dragged through forests, across deserts and over mountains as I searched for birds, and fortunately for me, they travelled without too many complaints.

Special thanks go to Peter Davidson who accompanied me on two major trips. Although not a birder he was often able to spot an elusive species, allowing me to concentrate on sketching.

I met helpful people on my travels and chance encounters with other birders often provided me with valuable local knowledge.

Thank you to Simon for designing my book, as expected you have done a great job and thanks to Clara for proof reading, she is the literate one in the family.

Finally many thanks go to Ian Langford of Langford Press who has undertaken to publish this book. Ever since I completed the US trips some years ago I have wanted to see this body of work in book form and with Ian's support the project has come to fruition.

Colorado - April.   Cinnamon & Blue-winged Teal

Foreword

One of the unfortunate trends of the 21st century is the loss of a sense of place. For over 50 years there has been a harmonization of culture into a sort of "instant pudding" world. This is a world that is sl ck, smooth, sweet and very convenient. It is covering the variety on our planet with interchangeable uniformity. It is therefore very refreshing to see in this book by Michael Warren a celebration of places that still remain in the world of nature.

I have long admired Michael and his art. He has evolved away from his earlier rhythmic "art nouveau" style but his work still shows a sense of design though more naturalistic than his earlier work. The fact that he is a very knowledgeable birder

comes through strongly in all his work. This is appropriate because birds in general are now literally the new canaries in the coal mine. They are not just an embellishment on an ecosystem. They are key players. It is essential that we pay attention to the standing of bird populations as an indication of what is happening to our environment.

Michael invites us to join him as he travels around North America capturing nature in particular places at particular times. It is well worth the trip.

Robert Bateman
Salt Spring Island, BC, Canada

California - August   Monterey Bay Pelagic trip.

Leatherback Turtle, Swordfish, Dall Porpoise and a nice array of seabirds.
Familiar species to me were Sooty Shearwater, Pomarine Jaeger & Sabines Gulls.
New ones were Black-footed Albatross, Pink-footed Shearwater, Cassin's & Rhinoceros Auklets.

ALASKA - July - Eagle beach - north of Juneau.
Seeing 'Eagle beach' on the map, I went there. To my amazement
there were 26 Bald Eagles present. Also an accompanying cast
of Bonaparte's & Glaucous-winged Gulls, and Northwestern Crows.

CONTENTS

Great Horned Owl at nest -
Colorado - April

Virginia - May

two beautiful Waterthrushes -
Northern & Louisiana

Introduction

In 1980 I designed a set of postage stamps featuring birds for the British Post Office. In those days' new issues of stamps used to be launched in New York for the American philatelic market. The launch event at the City Corp Building in New York brought me into contact with the late Jim Helzer, President and founder of Unicover Corporation, Cheyenne, Wyoming. The company printed collectables and stamps for the United States and many other countries. As a result of this meeting we embarked on a series of designs of conservation stamp sheetlets for the National Audubon Society. I was commissioned for this series for a total of fourteen years. Another major project involved painting a particular landmark in each of the fifty states, with an accompanying bird species. I elected to visit all these sites and spent time birding enroute. At the end of my travels I had sketchbooks full of drawings of many of the birds I had seen.

These state visits required numerous trips from the mid 1980's to mid 1990's, sometimes with the family, but also solo trips and with Peter Davidson. It was a fantastic experience to drive this vast and varied continent.

I was able to visit world famous sites such as the Grand Canyon, Mount Rushmore, the Hoh Rain Forest and Outer Banks of the Carolinas. Also lesser known places such as

Mount Sunflower, the highest point in Kansas, marked with a wrought iron sunflower, the cemetery at Bennington Old Church in Vermont, Halfbreed Lake in Montana and Dolly Sods in West Virginia. All the time I drew and kept notes of the birds I saw, not only for my work for Unicover and the Audubon Society but also for my own records. Some places I went to were renowned for the rich diversity of bird life such as Florida, Texas and Hawaii. More particular habitats like the Pawnee National Grasslands in Colorado were very rewarding with their speciality species and landscape.

America is amazingly varied from vast wildernesses to elegant cities like Denver, to the traditional ways that were experienced at Acoma Pueblo. We endured the most vivid and tumultuous thunderstorm in Kansas and spring in New Jersey saw changes of temperature from 70F to 30F in a matter of minutes. Much of what I saw has been portrayed through the pages of this book but a volume such as this cannot convey everything, so I have tried to capture a feel of the different states, the environment and the wealth of birdlife that can be found from 'sea to shining sea'. These travels turned out to be far more than just birding trips; they were about experiencing this amazing continent, its birds and other wildlife and I will never forget them.

California - August
A party of Acorn Woodpeckers in
a lower valley near Yosemite.

xxWhip-poor-will at dusk –
New Jersey – May.

ALABAMA

Alabama - May

Stormy springtime on the Gulf shore. A Barn Swallow
uses a low perch on the beach to sit out a downpour. Elsewhere
a group of migrant waders, Ruddy Turnstones, Sanderlings &
Semi-palmated Sandpipers. I find some Least Terns on another
section of shore. Common Nighthawks hunt dramatically against
darkened skies. In better weather a Great Crested Flycatcher,
Brown Pelicans with Laughing Gull, and a party of
feeding Cattle Egrets.

19

Alaska - July

Glacier Bay National Park provided stunning
scenery and a rich variety of wildlife.
Mountains and glaciers were the backdrop
to Hump-backed Whales amid flocks
of Red-necked Phalaropes.

Glorious tufted Puffins, Kittlitz's & Marbled
Murrelets.   Smart Pigeon Guillemots,
Horned Puffins & Common Murre.
Black Oystercatchers posed noisily on rocks.
A drake Harlequin Duck swam by a mini
iceberg, and a group of White-winged Scoters flew past.

ARKANSAS

Arkansas – April

The area of Hot Springs National Park was vivid with the sparkling greens of spring foliage, amid which I saw Yellow-throated Vireo & Baltimore Oriole. Warbler species seen included Yellow, Tennessee & Pine. Chimney Swifts flew overhead calling, and a Veery watched from cover. An open grassy area produced Northern Bobwhites, and near them a spectacular pair of Scissor-tailed Flycatchers.

23

Arizona - February
The awesome grandeur and scale of the Grand Canyon
was host to a Juniper Titmouse, such a plain and insignificant
bird. Also there were Scrub Jays and Mountain Chickadee.
In the magical Canyon de Chelly I watched a
beautiful Western Bluebird.

Rio Verde provided a good variety
of habitats, and some splendid birds along
the river valley. Brilliant Vermillion Flycatcher,
crisp black & white Black Phoebe, and Anna's Hummingbird,
all obvious on their perches. More discreet species in the area
included Black-throated Sparrow, Curve-billed Thrasher and
Ladder-backed Woodpecker.
   A Harris's Hawk surveyed the scene.

CALIFORNIA

California – August
The dramatic splendour of Yosemite & Sequoia National Parks
was wonderful. I watched a Pileated Woodpecker rubbing it's head on lichens
after bathing in a river. Vivid Western Tanager were in the trees. In more open
country a party of California Quail, Wrentit &
Lincoln's Sparrow.

26

High in Los Padres National Forest,
Rufous & Anna's Hummingbirds were whizzing
brilliantly around thistles. Two Mountain Quail appeared &
disappeared into thicker cover.

The coast at Point Pinos & Point Lobos was
excellent for Black Oystercatchers, Surfbirds,
Black & Ruddy Turnstones and Wandering Tattler.
All feeding amongst seaweed covered rocks.

Boreal Owl
Colorado - April

Male called as dusk fell, then flew in and
landed near nest cavity - Female emerged, they
flew away, then returned, and female squeezed back
into nesting hole. Male departed, then female
partially re-emerged and sat as light faded.

Colorado - July

Rocky Mountain National Park
is a wonderful area. Through it's
different zones and habitats, from
forested valleys to tundra, high peaks
and brilliant carpets of flowers.

Mountain Bluebirds & White-crowned Sparrow
stood out, but suβtle Brown-capped Rosy-finch
and American Pipit were very pleasing.
In higher, rockier more barren parts
there were parties of Clark's Nutcrackers. I watched
Horned Larks near a Marmot. At lower lusher
elevations, Broad-tailed Hummingbirds were
busy working abundant blooms.

CONNECTICUT

Connecticut - October

Blue Jay and Northern Cardinal complement the
many hues present in the foliage. Through the trees
A glimpse of a Downy Woodpecker, and a small party
of American Goldfinches. At dusk a Common Nighthawk
flicks past. In a marshy area are Green-winged Teal,
Red-winged Blackbirds and Common Grackle. A Catbird moves discreetly,
almost invisible in drab vegetation, in contrast to the brightness
of a American Redstart.

Delaware ~ October
A visit to Bombay Hook National Wildlife Refuge
by Delaware Bay. A splendid array
of birds were present around this superb
marsh. A distant mass of Snow Geese,
Northern Shovelers & Ruddy Duck.

This way just a background to the assembled waders.
American Avocets, Short-billed Dowitchers, Western & Pectoral
Sandpipers, Hudsonian & Marbled Godwits, Greater Yellowlegs.
Finally a familiar if unexpected sight to my English eyes, I found a
juvenile Ruff.

FLORIDA

Florida - February

Merritt Island is a large area of coastal marshland, protected by its proximity to the Kennedy Space Center. American White Pelicans hunt for food, there are loafing Wood Storks & Anhingas, also a group of Tricolored Herons and some Blue-winged Teal. The VAB is background to Black Skimmers. A juvenile Scissor-tailed Flycatcher & Common Snipe on muddy margins, and adult & juvenile Black-crowned Night Herons on a palm fringed perch.

GEORGIA

Georgia - February
The vast swampland of Okefenokee is a
huge wilderness area, home to many bird & animal
species. In wooded edges there are beautifully
plumaged Wood Ducks, and a Red-headed Woodpecker.

Huge open vistas, backed by
moss strewn cypresses, are home to Sandhill Cranes,
Ring-necked Ducks, Great Egrets and Northern Harrier.
    A Red-shouldered Hawk watches from it's perch
as Tree Swallows flit over water lilies.

Hawaii – June

A splendid array of seabirds in
the area of Kilauea Point. Black Noddy,
Brown & Red-footed Booby,
Great Frigatebird,
Red-tailed & White-tailed Tropicbird,
Wedge-tailed Shearwater &
Laysan Albatross.

Hawaii - May/June

Dramatic landscapes with strange and wonderful birds
All unfamiliar to European eyes. Volcanic steam rising from
black land, and beautiful plant forms with vivid flowers.
Birds included Hawaiian Goose, Apapane, I'iwi, Elepaio,
Hawaiian Thrush, Amakihi, Anianiau & Akepa.

Idaho - February

A winter wonderland, vast snow covered vistas etched by forests and mountains. Occasional areas of open water hosted Trumpeter Swans. On the rivers, waterfowl included Hooded Mergansers, Buffleheads, and Barrow's Goldeneyes, also American Dipper. On the forest edge were Black-billed Magpie and Mountain Chickadee, and finding food in more open areas, parties of Ravens and Snow Buntings.

Illinois — May

I visited the locality of Lake Chautauqua. This habitat where forest and water meet was excellent for many species. Red-headed & Red-bellied Woodpecker, White-breasted Nuthatch, Eastern Phoebe and Tree Swallows all found perches. Below a Spotted Sandpiper bobbed on debris. Mourning Doves were seen enroute, and an area of sandy prairie produced Indigo Bunting, Grasshopper & Lark Sparrows.

Indiana - May

Indiana Dunes State Park lies on the southern shore of Lake Michigan.
A splendid system of sand dunes leading in to other habitats, including
woodland and swampy areas. Northern Rough-winged Swallows & Eastern
Kingbird watched from perches. A pair of Blue-gray Gnatcatchers were nesting in
a tree fork.   Warblers included Palm, Magnolia & Black-throated Green.
Near water I also found Marsh Wren and Swamp Sparrow.

49

IOWA

Iowa - May.

The environs of DeSoto Lake provided a good
variety of water and farmland birds. The mix of
habitat a contrast to huge farmed areas. Black Terns
flew elegantly over the lake, a pair of Wood Ducks in a tree,
and a Blue-winged Teal quietly feeding. There were Common
Yellowthroat and Red-winged Blackbird. Away from the water
I saw Yellow-headed Blackbird, Eastern Meadowlark,
Common Grackle & House Wren.

Colorado - April
A dramatic rocky area.
Birds included Canyon Wren, Say's Phoebe.
Williamson's Sapsucker and White-throated swifts.

KANSAS

Kansas – July

High summer, vast harvested fields stretch to the horizon.
A golden haze, and darkening storm clouds. Flat can
be dramatic. A roadside fencepost is used by a Common Nighthawk
for a daytime snooze. Yellowheaded Blackbirds & Brown headed
Cowbirds work the stubble.

Other species in roadside vegetation included Western Meadowlark, Lark Buntings, Grasshopper Sparrow & Orchard Oriole. Seeking the vantage of higher plants & post were Western Kingbird & Loggerhead Shrike

Kentucky – May

I spent time in the area of Mammoth Cave National Park.
The woodlands, a glittering array of springtime greens, were alive with birds.
A Barred Owl peered from cover. Warblers included Black & White, Kentucky,
Chestnut-sided, Tennessee and Worm-eating. Near the river were
Common Yellowthroat & Yellow-breasted Chat. There was Red-eyed Vireo,
and at dusk I glimpsed a Chuck-will's-widow through the trees.

LOUISIANA

Louisiana – April
Glimpsed through the trees is Oakley
Plantation House, where legendary bird painter
John James Audubon worked. Summer Tanager and Northern
Parula were nearby. Not far from New Orleans there were
many bird species in and around the swamplands.
Mississippi Kites overhead, an array of warblers including
Prothonotary, Swainson's, Hooded & Kentucky. Brilliant
Painted Bunting and Scarlet Tanager, also
Dickcissel & Rose-breasted Grosbeak.

Maine - October

Dramatic coastlines, overlayed with atmospheric rain & mists.
Seas pounding on rocks. The Maine shore is a great place to
watch birds. Here I found numbers of Red-necked Grebes, counting
up to 33 in one place. Common & Arctic Loons slipped through
the grey waters. There were Black Guillemots, rafts of Eiders, and a few
surf Scoters. In a more sheltered, seaweedy bay, a stately Great
Blue Heron with a group of American Black Ducks.

Maryland - October

Blackwater wildlife Refuge is a vast tidal marsh. It teems with wild fowl. A Bald Eagle surveyed the scene as a Northern Harrier drifted past.

There were Great Egrets. Huge numbers of Canada Geese were flighting in to join others already present.
Large flocks of Mallard & Northern Pintails graced the open waters.

New Jersey – May
a glittering array of spring warblers –

MASSACHUSETTS

MASSACHUSETTS - October

The famous peninsular of Cape Cod is steeped in history.
The tower commemorating the Pilgrim Fathers peeps above scrub, sand dunes,
and shore. A few immature Northern Gannets drift across the sea. A gathering
of gulls is mostly Great Black-backed with some Ring-billeds. A female Merlin
rests from hunting, as a party of Horned Larks seek food amid the beach
debris. In a sheltered pool I watched four Greater Yellowlegs.

Several Northern Flickers worked the bleached trunks of dead trees. In lower vegetation were adult & 1st winter White-crowned sparrows, and Dark-eyed Juncos.

MICHIGAN

Michigan - May

Elegant Black Terns rest on a stump in a lake. A Bald Eagle drifts across the sky.
On the shore of Lake Michigan a Spotted Sandpiper with Point Sable lighthouse in
the background. The lake is vast, almost a sea. In wooded areas a splendid
Ruffed Grouse, and a Nashville Warbler. A large area of grassland provided an
interesting array of species. A very smart Bobolink, Short-eared Owl, Upland Sandpiper
& American Bittern. The latter three blending well in their surroundings.

MINNESOTA

Minnesota - May

A huge area of lakes and islands, the mix of bright water and dark trees providing some wonderful landscapes. I watched Common Loons swimming past. A pair of Common Mergansers loafed on rocks, nearby some Common Goldeneyes, all overseen by a Bald Eagle. A pair of Merlins occupied a promontory.
In the woodland were brilliant Yellow & Blackburnian Warblers amid the profusion of lichens. On the forest floor an Ovenbird.

Mississippi – May

From the splendid island beaches, through lush vegetation, to the
rich habitats of Yazoo National Wildlife Refuge. On the beach a Fish Crow
lived up to it's name, watched by Laughing Gulls and migrant Black-bellied Plover as
Magnificent Frigatebirds drifted past. Elsewhere Prothonotary Warbler, Green
Heron, Anhingas, Ruby-throated Hummingbirds, Dickcissel,
Brown Thrasher & Yellow-billed Cuckoo.

Missouri – May

Prairie country has it's own special landscape, soft rolling grassland and farmland, dotted with trees. There are many species of bird that have adapted to the habitats.

Greater Prairie Chickens, Northern Harrier, a young Loggerhead Shrike and Eastern Kingbird. I disturbed a small party of Northern Bobwhites. Nearby were American Goldfinches, and in the grasses Henslow's Sparrow, Dickcissel and a splendid Blue Grosbeak.

Colorado - April/May

A vast area of prairie, the Pawnee National Grassland
has a very special atmosphere and character. Birds included
Mountain Plovers, McCown's & Chestnut-collared Longspurs.

Montana - July

A hot summers day on the rolling plains by
the historic Custer National Monument.
Western Meadowlark song heard across the bleached
gravestones. Eastern Kingbird perched nearby.
En route a party of Cliff Swallows in riverside leaves,
and a Swainson's Hawk surveying the fields.

At Halfbreed Lake I found a wonderful assembly of waders.
American Avocets, lots of Wilson's Phalaropes, Greater & Lesser Yellowlegs,
Semi-palmated & Least Sandpipers. Beyond them Eared Grebes, and
a Prairie Falcon which flashed through causing
momentary panic.

NEBRASKA

Nebraska - July

In the North Platte river area I was fascinated by the Sandhills country. Sandy, grassy, softly rolling with occasional lakes. Upland Sandpipers & Long-billed Curlews were present in this unique habitat, the former frequently on fence posts.

Roadside there were attractive Lark Sparrows.

Birding along the river towards Scottsbluff,
I watched a Belted Kingfisher perched briefly on some
driftwood. Feeding around the sand banks were
Spotted Sandpipers & Killdeers.

Nevada- February

The arid, desert landscape hosts some
specialist species, including these splendidly gawky
Greater Roadrunners.   Rough-legged & Red-tailed Hawks watched
for prey, and a party of Gambel's quail scuttle past.
   Bewick's Wren and Hermit Thrush were present. On an area
of marsh I saw Common Mergansers, and a Golden Eagle hunted.

NEW HAMPSHIRE

New Hampshire - October

A glittering landscape, resplendent in
fall colours. A primary explosion of leaves
and reflections. On the lakes were Hooded Mergansers,
A couple of immature Surf Scoters with a Common Loon.
Also Ring-necked Duck & Belted Kingfisher.
Amongst the leaves, White-throated Sparrows
and American Robin. Above them a Red-breasted Nuthatch
near a party of noisy Blue Jays.

NEW JERSEY

New Jersey – October

At the southern tip of New Jersey lies Cape May.
A birding hotspot on the Atlantic flyway between the
ocean and Delaware Bay.   There were raptors.
Red-tailed Hawks, Turkey Vultures, Coopers & Sharp-shinned Hawks.
A Merlin took a Yellow-rumped Warbler & a magnificent juvenile
tundra Peregrine was hunting.

In marshy areas, Great Blue Heron, Red-winged Blackbird, Mallard & Black Duck formed a background to Pectoral, Stilt & Semi-palmated Sandpipers.

In vegetation a Hermit Thrush skulked. Above amid rich fall colours were Golden-crowned Kinglet & Yellow-rumped Warbler.

Florida — April

White-winged Dove, White-crowned Pigeon,
Caracara, Swallow-tailed Kite, Limpkin, Mottled Duck,
Purple Gallinule, Sora, Least & American Bitterns.

Most of these species are specialities
of this sub-tropical region.

New Mexico - February

The superb wildlife refuge of Bosque del Apache teemed
with birds. Dominant were the Snow Geese, but amongst them
were smaller numbers of Ross's Geese. Elegant Sandhill Cranes
strode about, and nearby I saw Neotropic Cormorants, Northern
Harrier, Bald Eagle and Marsh Wren. Away from the water a
party of Wild Turkeys moved through.
Later I visited the Acoma Pueblo. The dramatic
sandstone mesa was a splendid background to small parties
of Common Ravens.

New York - September
Jamaica Bay is a great place to watch birds, so near to
New York city. Here Glossy Ibis preen, a Green Heron
lurks in cover, as a party of American Wigeon drift past.
With the city on the horizon a black & white group features
Brants with Horned Grebes, and American Oystercatchers on the shore.
In nearby cover a Hermit Thrush, and Yellow-billed Cuckoo.

Later, visiting Montauk on
Long Island, I found a variety of migrant
birds. These included Nashville & Cape May
Warblers, and Baltimore oriole. Nearer the shore
I saw Palm Warblers as a Parasitic Jaeger
flew past over the surf.

NORTH CAROLINA

North Carolina – October

Cape Hatteras is part of the Outer banks barrier islands.
Ocean, beaches and salt marshes forming a
dramatic habitat.   Willets fed on the shore.
Brown Pelicans drifted elegantly past, and a
Yellow butterfly appeared momentarily above
feeding Sanderlings. In the marshes there
were Tundra Swans, Pied-billed Grebes
and a splendidly handsome group of
Boat-tailed Grackles.

North Dakota – August

The landscape at Theodore Roosevelt National
park was immediately attractive. Rich, vibrant
earth colours provided a background to many
bird species there. Burrowing Owls and
Gophers shared a space.

Brilliant Lazuli Bunting and American
Goldfinch glowed. A juvenile American Redstart
briefly in leaves. In lower cover I found Chipping
Sparrow, Black-headed Grosbeak & Spotted Towhee.
From a brushy area flushed some Sharp-tailed Grouse.
Two Golden Eagles on adjacent telegraph poles
was a spectacular sight.

OHIO

Ohio - May

Beautiful springtime woodlands above the Little Miami River.
Many species of birds could be seen and heard
including Swainson's & Wood Thrushes. A Pileated Woodpecker
foraged on the forest floor, an Eastern Wood-Peewee perched above
with food. Warblers included Yellow-rumped and the superb duo of
Blue-winged & Golden-winged. The reds of Tanagers,
both Summer and Scarlet contrasted
the abundant green foliage.

Florida - September
Magnificent Frigatebirds, Piping - Wilson's -
Semi-palmated & Snowy Plovers, Smooth-billed Ani,
Snail Kite, Carolina Wren, White Ibis, Roseate Spoonbills,
Yellow-crowned Night Heron, Reddish Egrets &
Little Blue Heron.

Oklahoma - May

Attracted by descriptions of the Salt Plains area, I found a unique habitat. The shimmering vista of salt etched mud, dotted with vegetation, provided a background to numerous bird species. American White Pelican, American Avocet, Wilson's Phalarope, Baird's Sandpiper, Snowy Plover & Franklin's Gull. A bushy tree held a colony of Little Blue Heron with many Cattle. Also in the tree were Wild Turkey, Orchard Oriole and Scissor-tailed Flycatcher.

103

Oregon - July

Crater Lake, huge, eerie, and intense blue,
lies in the caldera of a collapsed volcano. A dramatic
landscape in which to search for birds.
Three-toed Woodpeckers, a juvenile & adult, their heads mimicking
lichens, graced a pine. Clark's Nutcrackers, Cassin's Finches &
Pine Siskins were nearby. On a snowpatch, a handsome
Gray-crowned Rosy-Finch. In typical habitat, a Rock Wren
Later I visited the coast near Tillamook. Common Murres & Tufted Puffins
on the rocks, Western Gull with Killdeer on the beach.

PENNSYLVANIA

Pennsylvania - October.

Anticipating large and dramatic
raptor movements, my visit to
Hawk Mountain coincided with
low cloud! Just the local Turkey
vultures were present, also some
Dark-eyed juncos.

106

At Gettysburg,
beyond the enormous historic
significance of the site, I saw
beautiful Eastern Bluebirds.

Other birds in the area & enroute
included juvenile Red-headed
Woodpecker, Eastern Towhees,
Cardinal & Purple finches.

109

Rhode Island - October

A seascape with a scattering of ducks. Surf & Black Scoters with a
few Red-breasted Mergansers. Closer to the shore, Double-crested Cormorants
balanced on spray covered rocks. Some Sanderlings, pale in their winter
plumage, inhabited swathes of seaweed.

A Belted Kingfisher on a
Harbourside perch.

Away from the shore, amid
beautiful autumn foliage, were
Monarch Butterflies.

A Brown Creeper on a
tree trunk, a Song Sparrow
skulking in leaves and grasses.
This Northern Cardinal
vied for brightness with
the brilliant colours
of the leaves.

SOUTH CAROLINA

South Carolina - February
A pair of Bald Eagles with a nest. One bird
flew to nest with a small branch, and sat
holding it in it's beak.

A Pileated Woodpecker clings to a vine,
feeding on barries. Trailing Live oak branches,
dripping with Spanish Moss, were background to Northern
Flicker, Northern Cardinal & American Robin.
High in various trees there were Red-cockaded &
Red-bellied Woodpeckers, also a Brown-headed
Nuthatch on a fern covered branch.
Two species of Kinglet, Ruby-crowned &
Golden-crowned, worked through the
dense vegetation.

California - August   Monterey Harbour

California Sea Lions & Sea Otters. A host of birds occupying the
breakwater. Brown Pelicans, Brandt's Cormorants & Heermann's Gulls.

SOUTH DAKOTA

South Dakota – August

The iconic image of Mount Rushmore is truly impressive, a superb sight. Framed in conifers it was a great place to look for birds. Hairy Woodpecker, adult & juvenile Red-naped Sapsuckers & Red-breasted Nuthatch worked the trees. A juvenile Townsend's Solitaire occupied a high perch. Turkey Vultures drifted over, watched by an American Kestrel. Glimpses of Yellow-rumped Warblers amid pine branches, and lower down a Western Tanager emerged brightly from leaves.

Tennessee - April

Spring in the area of Reel Foot Lake provided many birding experiences. Rich in habitats it was a delight to explore. Here were contrasts such as Red-shouldered Hawk & Ruby-throated Hummingbird, Acadian Flycatcher & Cerulean Warbler. In deeper cover Red-headed Woodpecker, Wood Ducks, Barred Owl and Black & White Warbler. A Wild Turkey dashed for cover, and Indigo Buntings displayed their beauty against yellow flowers.

TEXAS

Texas - February
Two spectacular birding experiences here were displaying
Greater Prairie-Chickens and wintering Whooping Cranes. Many
other species were seen in this bird rich area, including Prairie Falcon,
Sprague's Pipit & Harris's Sparrow in the prairie area.
In other parts Ferruginous & White-tailed Hawks,
Blue-headed Vireo & Orange-crowned Warbler. In the coastal
marsh at Aransas a beautiful White-tailed Kite.

Utah - February

Winter in this rocky wilderness, brilliant, sharp & cold. A pair of Red Crossbills, Western Bluebird and Bushtits. A Red-tailed Hawk high above the canyon, and lower down Western Scrub-Jay, Rock Wren & Dark-eyed Junco. A Sage Thrasher in typical habitat. Along a river, through a dramatic canyon, a pair of American Dippers braved the icy water.

VERMONT

Vermont - October

Crisp blue skies and yellow leaves, foliage dying back
into many varieties of brown. Along the valley of a bubbling
stream, I found a Black-billed Cuckoo. Also in the area I
watched Purple Finches, Tufted Titmouse, a Winter Wren and
Black-capped Chickadee. On the edge of a town a small party of Cedar
Waxwings, White-breasted Nuthatch & a Mourning Dove.

Arizona - February
The Saguaro National Monument, a superb
desert panorama with spiky and bizarre plant shapes.
Birds here included Gila Woodpeckers, Cactus Wrens
everywhere, Pyrrhuloxia, Phainopepia, Canyon
Towhee & Inca Doves.

VIRGINIA

Virginia – October.

Monticello, built by Thomas Jefferson, is set on a hilltop in beautiful rolling Virginian landscape. In the gardens and grounds, I found a juvenile Yellow-bellied Sapsucker, Eastern Phoebe, Ruby-crowned Kinglet & Northern Mockingbird. Later I visited Assateague Island. This wonderful area is a barrier island with extensive

beaches, dunes & marshes. Home to
many species of birds, it also has a
population of wild horses. Here were
Great Egrets & Tricolored Herons,
and assembled in a group on the sands,
Caspian & Forster's Terns, Black Skimmers
& Black-bellied Plovers.

WASHINGTON

Washington - July
The Grandeur of Olympic National Park,
with snow capped mountains and vast forests,
was a superb sight.
There were Blue Grouse,

Olive-sided Flycatcher, Black-throated Gray &
Townsend's Warblers.
Hoh Rain Forest was a silent cathedral of trees,
draped with moss. Varied thrush and Chestnut-backed
Chickadee were there, also Steller's Jay. En route Wilson's Warbler
& Gray Jays. Descending to the dramatic wood strewn Rialto beach,
I was rewarded with Peregrine & Rock Sandpipers.

West Virginia - October -

Here is a seemingly endless landscape of hills,
with hardwood & conifer forests. In the areas of
Seneca Rocks & Dolly Sods, and Blackwater Falls there were
many habitats. Rocky outcrops, river valleys and
rich vegetation. A party of Cedar Waxwings
fed on abundant berries. Among other species
was a splendid Rose-breasted Grosbeak,
Swamp & White-throated Sparrows.
A Ruffed Grouse flashed through the brilliant
leaves past a Downy Woodpecker.

Wisconsin - May

Apostle Island: National Lakeshore lies on the edge of
Lake Superior. Here were Tree & Barn Swallows perched above
the beach. Inland a swampy, wooded area produced Yellow-rumped
and Black & White Warblers. A Northern Harrier skimmed the water, with a pair
of Blue-winged Teal nearby. A trio of Solitary Sandpipers waded against
woodland reflections. At the waters edge a Song Sparrow and in
drier cover I watched a Brown Thrasher.

WYOMING

Wyoming – July

Yellowstone National Park is a spectacular wilderness with many habitats. Violet-green Swallows against a cliff face. Osprey overlooking a waterfall, with American Dipper against the torrent below.

134

The geysers were remarkable, and the only species I found near them was a Killdeer.

A moose lazed behind a Gray Jay & a Townsend's Solitaire watched from high.

Grazing Buffalo moved slowly past a Chipping Sparrow. The dramatic Tetons were a superb backdrop to a family party of Trumpeter Swans.

Southern Texas including Rio Grande area - April

A wealth of species in this bird rich part of the state.
Fulvous & Black-bellied Whistling Duck, Great Kiskadee,
Altamira Oriole, Green & Ringed Kingfishers, Least Grebe,
Golden-fronted Woodpecker, White-tipped Dove, Hook-billed Kite, Plain Chachalaca
& Green Jay. Finally the amazing sight of huge number of
Broad-winged Hawks taking to the sky in the morning.

Brown Pelicans - Sanibel, Florida - September

Western Grebes – Colorado – April

Clapper Rail –
New Jersey – May

142

White-eyed Vireo - Florida - April

California - August.   Los Padres National Forest.
A male, one of three remaining wild individuals. First seen in
distant flight. Later found at a carcase, standing off as a Golden Eagle
fed. Afterwards took flight around valley, then flew overhead and away.